Cases from Management
Accounting Practice
Volume 5

Edited by

Michael A. Robinson, Ph.D.
Abilene Christian University

The American Accounting Association
(Management Accounting Section)

and

The National Association of Accountants
(Committee on Academic Relations)

Published by

National Association of Accountants
10 Paragon Drive, Montvale, NJ 07645-1760

Alice Watkins, Compositor
Pat Wickham, Typesetter
Mandel & Wagreich, Inc., Cover

Table of Contents

Foreword

This volume contains five cases involving current management accounting issues being confronted in practice. The cases describe actual situations faced by Libbey-Owens-Ford Co., Tektronix, Inc., and Stanadyne Diesel Systems. The cases were prepared for the Management Accounting Symposia Series sponsored by the National Association of Accountants' (NAA) Committee on Academic Relations and the Management Accounting Section of the American Accounting Association (AAA). The symposia series was established to increase the dialogue between the academic community and practicing management accountants.

The cases from the fifth Management Accounting Symposium are contained in this volume. The Rossford and United L/N cases were prepared by Professor Robert H. Colson of Case Western Reserve University and Mr. Mark MacGuidwin of Libbey-Owens-Ford Co. The Portables Group case was prepared from material presented by Mr. John W. Jonez and Mr. Michael A. Wright of Tektronix, Inc. The two Stanadyne Diesel Systems cases were prepared by Professor Carol J. McNair of the University of Rhode Island. All cases are meant to stimulate discussion of management accounting issues rather than to illustrate correct or incorrect practice.

Most of the costs of the symposia series are covered by the supporting companies. In addition, each supporting company is developing several cases for presentation in the series. Currently, the supporting companies include Borg-Warner, CSX, Ernst & Whinney, Johnson & Johnson, and Monsanto. We encourage your support in recruiting additional companies to join in our efforts.

The cases in this volume and the materials in the accompanying Instructor's Manual may be duplicated for classroom use. However, the materials may not be included in articles, books, or other publications without prior written consent from the National Association of Accountants.

More information on the case books or the symposia series may be obtained by contacting Hadassah Slominsky.

Ms. Hadassah Slominsky, CMA, CPA
Manager—Academic Relations
National Association of Accountants
10 Paragon Drive
Montvale, NJ 07645-1760
(201) 573-6306

The Rossford Plant

Having heard Robert Kaplan speak on some of the shortcomings of current cost accounting systems, I decided to undertake a review of the cost accounting system at our Rossford Plant. I was particularly concerned whether the overhead costs were being allocated to products according to the resource demands of the products. Costing our products accurately has become more important for strategic purposes because of pressures to unbundle sets of original equipment windows for the automakers.

Mark MacGuidwin, Corporate Controller
Libbey-Owens-Ford Co.

Background

Libbey-Owens-Ford Co. (L-O-F), one of the companies in the Pilkington Group, has been a major producer of glass in the United States since the turn of the century. Its Rossford Plant produces about 12 million "lites" of tempered glass per year. (A lite is a unit such as a rear window, which is called a "back lite," or a side window, which is called a "side lite.") The plant makes front door windows, quarter windows, back windows, and sunroofs. About 96 percent of the lites produced are sold to original equipment (OE) automotive customers; the remaining 4 percent are shipped to replacement depots for later sale to replacement glass wholesalers. Lite sizes range from .73 square feet for certain quarter windows to about 13 square feet for the back lite of a Camaro/Firebird. The average size is approximately four square feet.

The Rossford Plant is comprised of two production processes: float and fabrication ("fab"). The float process produces raw float glass, the raw material for automotive windows. Blocks of float glass are transferred to the fab facility, where lites are cut to size, edged, shaped, and strengthened. The final product is then inspected, packed, and shipped.

Parts of the Rossford Plant date to the founding of the company. Unlike other L-O-F plants, which were designed around the automated Pilkington float-tank process with computer controlled cutting and finishing operations, the Rossford Plant was designed for the older process of polishing plate glass to final products. Pilkington float-tanks were installed in the plant during the 1970s, and the cutting processes were substantially automated during the 1980s. However, the finishing processes have not yet been automated to the extent as at the other plants.

Mark MacGuidwin, Corporate Controller of L-O-F, and Ed Lackner, Rossford's Plant Controller, became concerned during 1987 about the cost allocation process at Rossford for several reasons. First, the process had not been critically evaluated since the automation of the cutting processes. Second, the overhead cost structure at Rossford differed dramatically from that of other L-O-F plants. A larger pool of indirect costs was allocated to equipment centers. Third, they had collected evidence that the cost allocation process at Rossford was not accurately assigning costs to units of product. And fourth, changes in the company's competitive environment were raising strategic issues that demanded accurate product cost information for pricing, product mix, and production scheduling purposes.

Relationship of Size to Profit

In his investigation, MacGuidwin discovered what he believed were two key observations made by the Vice Presidents of Engineering and Manufacturing. Historically in the automotive glass business, original equipment customers have purchased a complete set of windows for a car model from a single glass manufacturer. From the glass manufacturer's perspective it was therefore necessary that the markup on cost for the entire set, or bundle, of glass units be adequate for profitability. Despite the buying habits of these OE customers, firms in the industry quoted selling prices for individual units of glass within each set. As easy benchmarks, the selling prices were customarily set in proportion to the size in square feet of the units, with smaller lites priced lower than larger lites.

However, the cost of producing automotive glass is not related proportionately to the size of the unit produced. The production process involves two principal fabricating operations: cutting the unit from a larger block of glass, and then bending it to the necessary shape and strengthening it in a tempering furnace. Neither the cost of cutting nor the cost of tempering is proportional to the size of the unit produced. Only a limited number of units can be fed into either a cutting machine or a tempering furnace regardless of the size of the units, with little or no difference in feed rates or resource consumption related to size.

The joint effect of these two observations is an understanding in the glass industry of the average relationship between unit size and unit profit that is depicted in Figure 1-1. Margin percentages for passenger car lites are somewhat higher than the industry average.

Recent changes in the competitive structure of the OE automotive glass industry have led to the possibility of "unbundling" sets of windows. Major customers are considering not only allowing different manufacturers to supply units for the same car model (for example, windshields from one and rear windows from another) but also setting target prices based on the manufacturing costs of the units, a process already begun by General Motors. Under these circumstances, the costs reported by the accounting system for individual units of glass have strategic implications that were not relevant in the past.

Current Product Costing Process

Figure 1-2 shows the cost center groupings for the production process. The float and fabricating operations report to the same plant manager and have a common support staff. Raw glass is transferred from float to fab at standard variable plus standard fixed cost. (Profits are measured only at the point of sale of the finished product to the customer.) Direct labor and overhead costs are assigned to units of final product as follows:

(1) Direct labor costs are assigned to equipment centers (lines of machines in PC&E and furnaces in Tempering) based on standard crew sizes. Thus, a labor cost per equipment hour is developed for each of the several machines and furnaces based on crew sizes and standard wage and fringe benefit rates.

(2) Overhead costs, both variable and fixed, that are directly traceable to a specific equipment center are pooled to develop a rate per equipment hour for that center.

(3) A standard feed rate is established for each lite for each applicable cutting machine and furnace, and costs are applied to product based on costs per equipment hour/units fed per hour. (Feed rates to different tempering furnaces differ substantially.)

(4) General (indirect) plant overhead costs are allocated in two steps:

  (i) 20 percent of the total is allocated to the float process and 80 percent to fabricating, then

  (ii) the 80 percent allocated to fabricating is assigned to units of product at a flat rate per square foot (approximately $1.00 per square foot in 1987, adjusted for differing yield rates).

The costs classified as general plant overhead amount to 30 percent of the total indirect costs of the plant. General plant includes approximately 100 salaried employees involved in plant management, engineering, accounting, material control, pollution control, quality control, maintenance management, research and development, production management, and human resources. It also includes depreciation of equipment and buildings not assigned to operating departments, property taxes and insurance, general plant maintenance, and post retirement costs.

MacGuidwin decided to limit his initial analysis to the automotive glass fabricating facility at the Rossford Plant. He and Lackner were confident that the process of assigning costs to units of raw float glass was sufficiently accurate. They also believed that the direct costs of labor and overhead associated with the PC&E and Tempering Furnace equipment centers were being properly attached to units of product based on the units' standard feed rates per hour. The rates had been set with downtime assumptions intended to cover mechanical and electrical problems, stockouts, and part changeovers.

"On the whole, Ed Lackner and I felt pretty good about what we were discovering," commented MacGuidwin. "Over two-thirds of the costs of the plant were being assigned to units of product based on metered usage of our two constraining resources, machine time in the PC&E center and furnace time in the Tempering center."

"On the other hand," Lackner pointed out, "we had a potential problem with our general plant costs. For years we had been assigning them to units produced based on square footage. We knew that this allocation base didn't capture activities that were driving the overhead costs, but we didn't know whether the allocation process was substantially distorting the final product costs. Until recently it didn't matter how these costs were allocated because unit price/cost differentials did not enter into any strategic decisions."

Alternative Allocation Method

The allocation of general plant overhead costs between float and fab seemed reasonable to the two Controllers. They analyzed a number of factors that could have been driving the allocation, including the number of hourly employees, the space occupied, and the variable costs incurred. They also interviewed managers concerning where time was spent by employees in the overhead base. All indicators pointed to the appropriateness of assigning 20 percent of the general plant costs to float and 80 percent to fab.

"The principal outcome of our analysis was to propose and implement on a test basis an alternative method for re-allocating the 80 percent allocated to fab," explained MacGuidwin. "Under the old method we allocated a flat rate per square foot produced. This might be reasonable if each square foot of glass costs the same to make in the PC&E and Tempering departments. However, we knew from our production engineers and from our own tracking of direct costs in those cost centers that this was just not the case."

To test an alternative allocation method, MacGuidwin and Lackner chose four parts with the following characteristics:

(1) a small, high volume, low profit margin part (Truck Vent);

(2) a small, high volume, moderate profit margin part (Passenger Car Rear Quarter Window);

(3) a large, high volume, moderate profit margin part (Passenger Car Front Door); and

(4) a large, moderate volume, high profit margin part (Passenger Car Back Lite, Heated).

As indicated in the following table, the direct costs of fabricating these parts differ substantially:

Part	Square Feet Per Unit	Cost Per Square Foot Cutting	Furnace
Truck Vent	.77	$2.870	$1.676
Passenger Car Rear Quarter	.73	1.494	3.312
Passenger Car Front Door	5.03	.340	.634
Passenger Car Back Lite	7.07	.206	.682

The input measure selected as the basis for allocating general plant overhead costs to units of product was the most scarce (bottleneck) resource in the facility—time spent in the tempering furnaces. The production plan indicated a furnace capacity of 48,500 hours per year. Dividing the portion of the costs assigned to fab by the furnace capacity resulted in a rate of $503 per furnace hour.

Using the feed rates of the individual pieces, MacGuidwin was able to compute a new standard cost for each of the four products. Figure 1-3 shows the standard cost per square foot, the cost per lite, and the gross margin percentage of each product under both the old and new methods of allocating general plant overhead. The Corporate Controller was pleased with the results:

> Although the results shown for the four products are not as dramatic as I've seen for some manufacturers, they do indicate a need to rethink and reanalyze our cost allocation system. Basically, the new method of allocating general plant overhead represents more closely what the Engineering and Manufacturing Vice Presidents were telling me about cost incurrence. The old system allocated a large pool of indirect costs equally to output, whereas the new system makes some attempt to associate those costs with the resource demands placed on our productive capacity by individual products. The old method clearly distorted our product costs. The new method should work better as long as we produce at plant capacity.

Required:

(1) What is the cost object before the change in the product costing system? After the change? Why did MacGuidwin and Lackner change the focus of the system?

(2) What are the characteristics of a good product costing system?

(3) How do the process control and product costing functions of Rossford's cost accounting system interact? What conversion costs are treated as direct product costs in the system?

(4) In your opinion, is the new allocation method for general plant costs better than the old method? Why or why not?

FIGURE 1-1

Unit Size/Profit Relationship

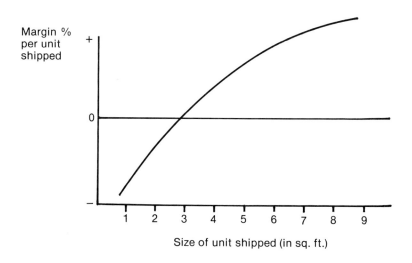

Margin % per unit shipped

Size of unit shipped (in sq. ft.)

FIGURE 1-2

Production Cost Centers

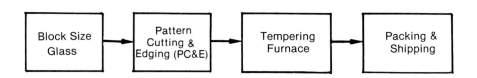

Block Size Glass → Pattern Cutting & Edging (PC&E) → Tempering Furnace → Packing & Shipping

FIGURE 1-3

Unit Data Under Old and New Allocation Methods

Truck Vent

	Old		New	
	Amount	Percent	Amount	Percent
Cutting	$2.870	47	$2.870	42
Furnace	1.676	27	1.676	24
General Plant	1.020	17	1.740	25
All Other Costs	0.566	9	0.566	8
Std. Cost Per Sq. Ft.	$6.132	100	$6.852	100
Sq. Ft. Per Lite	0.770		0.770	
Cost Per Lite	$4.722		$5.276	
Selling Price	$2.820		$2.820	
Gross Margin (Percent)	(67)		(87)	

Passenger Car Front Door

	Old		New	
	Amount	Percent	Amount	Percent
Cutting	$0.340	12	$0.340	14
Furnace	0.634	23	0.634	25
General Plant	1.036	38	0.800	32
All Other Costs	0.716	26	0.716	29
Std. Cost Per Sq. Ft.	$2.726	100	$2.490	100
Sq. Ft. Per Lite	5.030		5.030	
Cost Per Lite	$13.712		$12.525	
Selling Price	$16.820		$16.820	
Gross Margin (Percent)	18		26	

Passenger Car Rear Quarter

	Old		New	
	Amount	Percent	Amount	Percent
Cutting	$1.494	21	$1.494	16
Furnace	3.312	47	3.312	36
General Plant	1.022	14	3.020	33
All Other Costs	1.266	18	1.266	14
Std. Cost Per Sq. Ft.	$7.094	100	$9.092	100
Sq. Ft. Per Lite	0.730		0.730	
Cost Per Lite	$5.179		$6.637	
Selling Price	$6.680		$6.680	
Gross Margin (Percent)	22		1	

Passenger Car Back Lite

	Old		New	
	Amount	Percent	Amount	Percent
Cutting	$0.206	5	$0.206	6
Furnace	0.682	18	0.682	20
General Plant	1.064	28	0.674	20
All Other Costs	1.810	48	1.810	54
Std. Cost Per Sq. Ft.	$3.762	100	$3.372	100
Sq. Ft. Per Lite	7.070		7.070	
Cost Per Lite	$26.597		$23.840	
Selling Price	$56.120		$56.120	
Gross Margin (Percent)	53		58	

7

The United L/N Plant

We never imagined that we'd ever be looking at the type of costing issues at our United L/N Plant that have now become apparent. The plant design was engineered from the beginning as a state-of-the-art production process that would avoid most of the traditional problems. Now we're in the process of taking a second look.

Ken Marvin
Director, Planning and Control
OE Business Unit
Libbey-Owens-Ford Co.

Background

Libbey-Owens-Ford Co. (L-O-F), one of the companies in the Pilkington Group, has been a major producer of glass in the United States since the turn of the century. Its newest plant, United L/N, began producing glass products in November 1987. Located in Kentucky, United L/N is a joint venture between L-O-F and a Japanese company, Nippon Sheet Glass.

Unlike the Rossford Plant, which produces the raw float glass used in its fabrication process, United L/N is a fabrication plant only. The organization of the plant reflects the just-in-time, pull through philosophy. The production process is fully automated, requiring no human intervention from beginning to end. Very high quality and minimal scrap were expected to be the norm.

L-O-F treats the Rossford Plant as a standard cost center, but United L/N is organized as a strategic business unit (SBU). SBUs are evaluated on profit as well as cost control and other goals. The company charges United L/N Rossford's standard manufacturing cost for raw glass transferred between the two plants, whereas transfer prices between SBUs are usually negotiated by their managements.

Fabrication Process and Plant Design

The steps in the fabrication process are essentially the same as at other L-O-F facilities. First, the raw glass goes through pattern cutting where it is

9

trimmed to the basic shape of the lite (window) it will become. Second, the cut pattern is edged. Third, the edged pattern goes through a furnace where it is formed (bent to shape) and tempered. Fourth, the final product is inspected, packed, and shipped.

The principal difference between United L/N's process and the fabrication process of traditional plants lies in the organization of these discrete steps. At the Rossford Plant, for example, pattern cutting and edging, tempering, and packing and shipping are treated as individual cost centers and are physically separated. Each department creates a work-in-process inventory, which is periodically moved to the next stage in the process. The next stage in most cases is located in a different section of the plant. Also, all processes at Rossford require human participation.

By contrast, United L/N's fabrication process is entirely in-line and automated. Raw glass from Rossford and other plants arrives packed on special racks that are designed for United L/N's automated loading process. (The racks are also designed to protect the raw glass from damage between the shipping plant and the receiving area.) The glass has been inspected at the shipping plant to determine that each piece meets the specifications of the fabrication process.

A forklift operator loads racks of glass at the beginning of one of United L/N's two production lines. From that point on, the entire process is operated through a numerical control computer system. Human intervention occurs only during planned downtime periods when the line undergoes preventive maintenance, when a problem stops the line's progress, and when finished pieces are inspected prior to packing. Glass is continuously pulled through the process, so that ideally there should be no idle work-in-process inventory.

A small team of operators monitors the process, performs regular preventive maintenance, changes the computer settings for different lites, and makes unscheduled repairs as needed.

Product Costing System

The product costing system at United L/N is very straightforward compared to those of less automated L-O-F plants. Overhead costs associated with handling, storing, protecting, and accounting for work-in-process inventories are dramatically lower. The major components of cost include short-term fixed operating costs, labor costs of the operating teams, and the transfer prices of raw glass from other plants.

Because the entire process is automated and in-line, the feed rate is constant across all sub-processes for each individual lite being fabricated. The costing system consequently was designed as one large pool, which is assigned to units based on standard input prices and standard feed rates. The system allows for standard levels of downtime and anticipated yields. Products are not charged for either planned downtime or planned scrap, which were expected to be minimal due to the care with which the plant was designed, engineered, and monitored.

Production and Costing Problems

"It wasn't long before we began experiencing problems with our yields," commented Ken Marvin, Planning and Control Director of L-O-F's Original Equipment Business Unit. "At first we thought that the problems would be confined to adjusting and learning about the automated process. We thought that as we gained experience with it we could solve our difficulties without introducing more complicated costing mechanisms."

One of the first difficulties encountered was keeping the furnaces on the two lines working efficiently. Each one was designed to work perfectly when a certain number of glass pieces were being fired, a certain number were on the threshold entering the furnace, and a certain number were leaving it.

"In our traditional plants we stockpile pieces in front of the furnaces so that we can keep them filled to their optimal levels when forming and tempering," Marvin explained. "However, the United L/N lines were designed with no accumulators in front of the furnaces to keep them running efficiently at all times. For any number of reasons there might be gaps in the lines as they enter the furnaces. Partly because of these gaps and the resulting imperfect furnace operations, we have had unacceptably high scrap variances. Of course, scrap decreases the plant's yield.

"From the United L/N point of view the problem with scrap is caused by imperfections in the raw glass rather than by problems with the process. The plant's management therefore believes that the scrap variance should be charged to the shipping plants (including Rossford). Shipping plant managers, on the other hand, believe that the charge-back, even if appropriate (which remains an issue), is much too high. United L/N's costing system costs every piece as if it goes through the entire process rather than dropping out at, for example, pattern cutting or edging stages."

Another factor contributing to furnace inefficiency and ineffectiveness is that a line sometimes goes down unexpectedly because of a problem in pattern cutting or edging. The plant then incurs the opportunity costs associated both with having an empty tempering furnace and with having to reset the furnace after it has been empty during periods of time when it was programmed to be full.

"We have been tracking all sorts of variances trying to get some insights into the effects on costs of the kinks in the process," continued Marvin. "We calculate a combined materials usage and spending variance, a downtime variance, a throughput variance, and a scrap (yield) variance. However, all of them are valued on the basis of costs of the entire production process rather than on the value added to the stages of production where problems occur. Now we're reevaluating the design of our costing system at United L/N, especially in light of the ongoing negotiations with Rossford and other shipping plants."

Required:

(1) As a member of the Rossford Plant negotiating team, what would be your position regarding the proper treatment of the United L/N scrap variance? As a member of the United L/N team?

(2) How could United L/N's management determine the specific causes of defects (for example, bad glass or defective cutting, edging, or tempering operations) in units that are scrapped at the plant? What are the implications for the product costing system?

(3) What could be done to solve the problems with furnace inefficiency and ineffectiveness that Ken Marvin discussed? What are the probable effects of your suggestion(s)?

The Portables Group

Background

Tektronix, Inc., headquartered in Portland, Oregon, is a world leader in the production of electronic test and measurement instruments. The company's principal product since its founding in 1946 has been the oscilloscope (scope), an instrument that measures and graphically displays electronic signals. The two divisions of the Portables Group produce and market high- and medium-performance portable scopes.

Tektronix experienced almost uninterrupted growth through the 1970s based on a successful strategy of providing technical excellence in the scope market and continually improving its products in terms of both functionality and performance for the dollar. In the early 1980s, however, the lower-priced end of the division's medium-performance line of scopes was challenged by an aggressive low-price strategy of several Japanese competitors. Moving in from the low-price, low-performance market segment in which Tektronix had decided not to compete, these companies set prices 25 percent below the U.S. firm's prevailing prices. Rather than moving up the scale to more highly differentiated products, the group management decided to block the move.

The first step was to reduce the prices of higher-performance, higher-cost scopes to the prices of the competitors' scopes of lower performance. This short-term strategy resulted in reported losses for those instruments. The second step was to put in place a new management team whose objective was to turn the business around. These managers concluded that, contrary to conventional wisdom, the Portables Group divisions could compete successfully with foreign competition on a cost basis. To do so, the divisions would have to reduce costs and increase customer value by increasing operational efficiency.

Production Process Changes

The production process in the Portables Group divisions consisted of many functional islands, including etched circuit board (ECB) insertion, ECB assembly, ECB testing, ECB repair, final assembly, test, thermal cycle, test/QC, cabinet fitting, finishing, boxing for shipment, and shipment. The new management team consolidated these functionally-oriented activities into integrated production lines in open work spaces that allow visual control of the entire production area. Parts inventory areas were also placed parallel to production lines so that at each work station operators would be able to pull their own parts. This in essence created an early warning system that nearly eliminated line stoppages due to stockouts.

Additional steps that were taken in the early to mid 1980s to solve managerial and technical problems include implementation of just-in-time (JIT) delivery and scheduling techniques and total quality control (TQC), movement of manufacturing support departments into the production area, and implementation of people involvement (PI) techniques to move responsibility for problem solving down to the operating level of the divisions. The results of these changes were impressive: substantial reductions in cycle time, direct labor hours per unit, and inventory, and increases in output dollars per person per day and operating income. The cost accounting group had dutifully measured these improvements, but had not effectively supported the strategic direction of the divisions.

Cost Accounting System

Direct Material and Direct Labor

Figure 3-1 shows the breakdown of the total manufacturing cost of the newest portable scopes produced with the latest technologies. In most cases, material and labor are easily traced to specific products for costing purposes. Prior to the mid 1980s, however, the divisions' attempts to control direct labor had been a resource drain that actually *decreased* productivity.

There were approximately twenty-five production cost centers in the Portable Instruments Plant. Very detailed labor efficiency reports were prepared monthly for each cost center and each major step in the production process. In addition, an efficiency rating for each individual employee was computed daily. Employees reported the quantity of units produced and the time required to produce them, often overestimating the quantity produced to show improved efficiency against continually updated standards. The poor quality of collected data resulted in semi-annual inventory write-downs when physical and book quantities were compared.

"The inadequacy of our efficiency reporting system became clear when we analyzed one of our new JIT production lines," commented Michael Wright, Financial Systems Application Manager. "On a JIT manufacturing line, once the excess inventory has been flushed out, it is essentially impossible for any person to work faster or slower than the line moves. However, if one person on the line is having a problem, it immediately becomes apparent because the product flow on the line stops. Corrective action is then taken, and the line is started up again.

"On that line, the system told us that the efficiency of each of the workers was decreasing. However, stepping back from the detail of the situation allowed us to look at the overall picture. We found that the costs

14

incurred on the line were going down and its product output was going up. Obviously, it was becoming more, not less, efficient."

The quantity of direct labor data collected and processed also was a problem. Production employees often spent twenty minutes per day completing required reports when they could have been producing output. Additionally, the accounting staff was processing 35,000 labor transactions per month to account for what amounted to 3 percent of total manufacturing cost. "Transactions cost money," observed John Jonez, Group Cost Accounting Manager, "and lots of transactions cost lots of money."

In response to these problems, the group accounting staff greatly simplified its procedures. It abandoned the measurement of labor performance for each operation, and greatly reduced the number of variances reported. The number of monthly labor transactions fell to less than 70, allowing the staff to spend more time on overhead allocation and other pressing issues.

Overhead

The product costing system allocated all manufacturing overhead costs to products based on standard direct labor hours. A separate rate was computed for each manufacturing cost center. This system led to rapidly increasing rates; the direct labor content of the group's products had been continually decreasing for years, while overhead costs were increasing in absolute terms.

"Because the costing system correlated overhead to labor, our engineers concluded that the way to reduce overhead costs was to reduce labor," commented Jonez. "The focus of cost reduction programs therefore had been the elimination of direct labor. However, most of this effort was misdirected, because there was almost no correlation between overhead cost incurrence and direct labor hours worked. Our system penalized products with proportionately higher direct labor, but it wasn't those products that caused overhead costs. We proved that. We attacked direct labor and it went down, but at the same time overhead went up.

"We therefore knew that we needed a new way to allocate overhead. More fundamentally, we needed a way for the cost accounting system to support the manufacturing strategy of our group. The objective was clear—to provide management with accounting information that would be useful in identifying cost reduction opportunities in its operating decisions as well as provide a basis for effective reporting of accomplishments."

Approach to Method Change

Initial Steps

The first step taken by Wright and Jonez in developing a new overhead allocation method was to establish a set of desirable characteristics for the method. They decided that it must accurately assign costs to products, thus providing better support for management decisions than the old method. It must support the JIT manufacturing strategy of the Portables Group. It also must be intuitively logical and easily understandable by management. And finally, it must provide information that is accessible by decision makers.

The next step was to interview the engineering and manufacturing managers who were the primary users of product cost information. These users were asked, "What is it that makes your job more difficult? What is it that makes certain products more difficult to manufacture? What causes the production line to slow down? What is it that causes overhead?" The answers to these questions were remarkably consistent—there were too many unique part numbers in the system. This finding revealed a major flaw in the ability of the direct labor-based costing method to communicate information critical for cost-related decisions. Manufacturing managers realized there were substantial cost reduction opportunities through the standardization of component parts, but there was no direct method to communicate this idea to design and cost-reduction engineers who made part selection decisions.

Although difficult to quantity, some costs are associated with just carrying a part number in the database. Each part number must be originally set up in the system, built into the structure of a bill of materials, and maintained until it is no longer used. Moreover, each part must be planned, scheduled, negotiated with vendors, purchased, received, stored, moved, and paid for. Having two parts similar enough that one could be used for both applications requires unnecessary duplication of these activities, and therefore unnecessary costs.

Standardizing parts results in several indirect benefits. Fewer unique part numbers usually means fewer vendors and greater quality of delivered parts. It also means smoother JIT production, fewer shutdowns of manufacturing lines, and greater field reliability. These observations led to a preliminary consensus on the need to develop a product costing method that would quantify and communicate the value of parts standardization.

Cost Analysis

"To confirm our assessment," stated Jonez, "we segmented the total manufacturing overhead cost pool. The costs of all cost centers comprising the pool were categorized as either material-related or conversion-related based upon rules developed in conjunction with operating managers. [See Figure 3-2.]

"Material-related costs pertain to procurement, scheduling, receiving, incoming inspection, stockroom personnel, cost-reduction engineering, and information systems. Conversion-related costs are associated with direct labor, manufacturing supervision, and process-related engineering. Application of the rules resulted in an approximately 55/45 split between material overhead (MOH) and conversion overhead (COH). This finding further confirmed the inadequacy of the existing method, which applied all overhead based on direct labor.''

The accounting analysts decided to focus their initial efforts on the MOH pool. To improve their understanding of the composition of the pool and thus assist them in developing a method for its allocation, Wright and Jonez consulted operating managers and further segmented it into:

(1) Costs due to the value of parts,

(2) Costs due to the absolute number of parts used,

(3) Costs due to the maintenance and handling of each different part number and

(4) Costs due to each use of a different part number.

The managers believed that the majority of MOH costs were of type (3). The costs due to the value of parts (1) and the frequency of the use of parts (2 and 4) categories were considered quite small by comparison.

The analysts therefore concluded that the material-related costs of the Portables Group would decrease if a smaller number of different part numbers were used in its products. This cost reduction would result from two factors. First, greater volume discounts would be realized by purchasing larger volumes of fewer unique parts. Second, material overhead costs would be lower. "It was the latter point that we wanted our new allocation method to focus on,'' commented Wright.

"Our goal,'' continued Jonez, "was to increase customer value by reducing overhead costs. Our strategy was parts standardization. We needed a tactic to operationalize the strategy.''

Required:

(1) Using assumed numbers, develop a cost allocation method for material overhead (MOH) to quantify and communicate the strategy of parts standardization.

(2) Explain how use of your method would support the strategy.

(3) Is any method which applies the entire MOH cost pool on the basis of one cost driver sufficiently accurate for product decisions in the highly competitive portable scope markets? Explain.

(4) Are MOH product costing rates developed for management reporting appropriate for inventory valuation for external reporting? Why or why not?

FIGURE 3-1

Manufacturing Costs

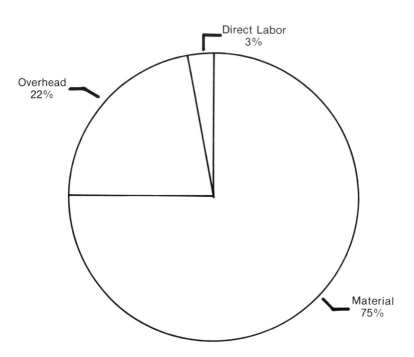

FIGURE 3-2

**Rules for Overhead Segmentation
by Cost Center Classification**

(1) *Production.* The overhead costs of any cost center containing direct labor employees are assigned 100 percent to the COH pool.

(2) *Group/Division/Product Group Staff.* The total costs of any manufacturing staff cost center are assigned 50 percent to the COH pool and 50 percent to the MOH pool.

(3) *Group/Division/Product Group Support.* The total costs of any manufacturing support cost center (e.g., Material Management or Information Systems) are assigned 100 percent to the MOH pool.

(4) *Manufacturing Cost-Reduction Engineering.* The total costs of any cost-reduction engineering cost center are assigned 100 percent to the MOH pool.

(5) *Manufacturing Process-Related Engineering.* The total costs of any process-related engineering cost center are assigned 100 percent to the COH pool.

Case 4

Stanadyne Diesel Systems (A)

The problem facing most manufacturers is that their facilities are not structured to meet the demands of a global marketplace, and there are many roadblocks that make the transition to an automated factory difficult. One of the most important, but least understood of these roadblocks is current cost management systems. These systems do not provide companies with the financial information necessary to manage the transition to a factory of the future.

James Brimson, 1986

Background

Standadyne Diesel Systems manufactures and markets complex precision metal products and components of foreign and domestic industrial consumer goods. Its major products include diesel pumps, nozzles, fuel heaters, mechanical tappets, and related products used in the production of industrial and automotive diesel engines.

Stanadyne has experienced roller-coaster demand for its products in the 1980s. During the gasoline crisis, automobile manufacturers and consumers alike turned to diesel-powered automobiles to combat the high cost of gasoline. In conjunction with a major automobile manufacturer, the company embarked on a program of rapid expansion of production capacity to meet projected demand. Production peaked in 1984. The Plant Manager, Gene Brady, put it this way:

At the peak of production, we just couldn't hire people fast enough. Every day the plant foreman would run up to personnel to see if any qualified people had come in to interview. We were taking just about anybody, just to make sure we could keep up with orders. And, we were managing by the seat of our pants. The growth was just too fast—everything was out of control.

This situation was not long-lived, though. Americans never truly came to love the diesel engine, especially the one containing Stanadyne parts. Due to quality problems with other components of the engine, the number and frequency of breakdowns put the product into an early grave. For the automobile manufacturer, a loss was incurred. For Stanadyne, it meant not only a substantial, and perhaps fatal, loss of business, but also a downturn exacerbated by extreme overcapacity. The company had invested a substantial amount in expanded capacity for which there was then no need.

A Unique Culture

Stanadyne is the direct descendent of a traditional metal-working job shop. In its early years it made various types of screws and bolts, using machinery quite advanced for its time. When talking about the company, managers refer to the impact the ''job shop'' mentality continues to have on the daily operations of the business.

Stanadyne has a strong, ingrown culture. This culture has its roots in its founders—individuals who worked as machinists prior to making the leap into owning their own business. Before its takeover by a conglomerate in 1987, the firm was able to boast a history of consistent promotion through the ranks. In fact, every president prior to 1987 started in the plant as a day worker. It is not a company characterized by ties and jackets, but rather by dirty hands and hard work.

The focus on promotion from within makes Stanadyne a unique company. Managers, from top to bottom, are ''lifers.'' Most have never worked for another company. These individuals really know the company and its capabilities, and are willing to go the extra mile to ensure that high quality products are produced and shipped on time. Because of the long-standing tenure of the managers, most decision-making is done through meetings and informal networks, rather than through mandates from the top. It is a fully participating management in which everyone has a say in the process. This is reflected in the fact that every management employee with any tie to daily production attends an 8:00 a.m. meeting during which problems are aired and resolved in open forum.

The down side of Stanadyne's culture is the very informality that keeps its employees involved. Very few operating procedures are written down. Individuals make the organization run; if one person is out, the entire system slows down. Additionally, when problems occur people rather than new practices or approaches are looked to for solutions. In this loose organizational structure, individuals who take action to solve problems often do not pass along the information to others who could enact long-term solutions.

Just-in-Time Technology: A White Knight

Given the high costs that were embedded in the facility itself, Stanadyne had to find a way to produce a low marginal cost injector of high quality if lost sales were to be recouped. Facing stiff competition for its diesel injectors abroad, and no domestic market for automotive injectors, the company

20

sought a new approach to gain a competitive edge.

In desperate straits, management began to listen to individuals in the firm who believed that Just-in-Time (JIT) manufacturing was the approach that Stanadyne needed. Two managers played a key role in bringing the JIT approach to the company: Bill Holbrook, then the V.P. of Materials, and Jeff Anderson, who directly managed the materials planning group. Working together, Holbrook and Anderson crafted a plan for implementing the approach. They convinced their fellow managers of the benefits of JIT and related quality control techniques, and the group pursued implementation with a vengeance.

In the implementation phase, approximately 60 percent of the plant was reorganized into JIT cells, 20 percent into "Islands of Automation" (e.g., numerically controlled machines), and the remainder along functional lines. The cells themselves range from highly sophisticated robotic lines employing Kanban, electronic sensing devices and various forms of on-line quality control to others created simply by bringing old machines together. After cells were created, management relied on production personnel to reorganize their processes to achieve further efficiency gains in the production of components and subassemblies.

Due to the implementation of JIT techniques and additional efforts to standardize its products, Stanadyne has trimmed inventories from a high of $37 million in 1984 to $15 million in 1988. This has translated into a reduction of 19,000 square feet of inventory on the plant floor. Improved quality also has been achieved, with scrap down an average of 25 percent per year since 1984 to a 1988 level of $500,000, while the number of quality control inspectors has dropped substantially, down to 15 from a high of 60. Management believes that fully 80 percent of the benefits of implementing JIT methods have resulted from moving machines together, eliminating move and queue elements of process time.

Management Accounting in a JIT Setting

A key aspect of the JIT approach is the recognition of interdependence in the manufacturing process—that is, that the entire process is linked, and is constrained by the slowest machine or work center. This is common sense, but the traditional manufacturing literature stresses reducing the impact of interdependence by putting inventory buffers between machines. By contrast, the JIT approach considers inventory to be an area of waste to be eliminated.

For the management accounting system, several changes are suggested by the move to JIT. First, enhanced visibility and product-flow throughput lead to more emphasis on operational control measures. This is reflected in the use of various measures to monitor total processing time versus the time elapsed from raw materials release to finished goods. It is also reflected in control systems that match the level of controllability. The supervisor on the plant floor can control only direct costs; upper management is responsible for indirect items. Everyone's goal is to remove waste and to gain better control of the plant's processes.

Additional changes occurring in practice include the simplification of inventory tracking (e.g., backflushing), the use of rolling averages of actual costs to monitor continuous improvement performance goals, and more widespread use of two-stage allocation processes that assign indirect costs to products based on consumption of resources instead of the use of overhead rates to spread the costs. Overall, the result is more focused and effective management accounting information systems that match the needs of the various decision-makers within firms.

What has been the impact of JIT implementation on the management accounting system at Stanadyne? The company has made major changes in its basic plant control system. Two of the primary modifications are: (1) replacement of traditional standards-based control reports with "Business Reports," and (2) utilization of "checkbooks" for managing the plant floor. Both of these changes reflect the Controller's desire to match reporting formats with controllability criteria by focusing the attention of those who can affect change on the areas under their control. Additionally, the Controller continues to pursue the replacement of standard costs with actuals for operational control and performance evaluation, and to push this control to the lowest feasible level in the organization.

Business Reports

Stanadyne has replaced its traditional full absorption cost-based reports with a contribution margin reporting format. A typical report generated by the new system is presented in Figure 4-1, whereas a traditional standards-based report, which is still generated by Stanadyne to meet corporate requirements, is shown in Figure 4-2. Maintenance of this dual system is viewed by Mike Boyer, the Controller, as follows:

> If we can't integrate with the financial accounting system we'll
> set up two information systems, because we have to know what
> it truly costs us to run the business.

The key characteristic of the revised management accounting system used by the plant is the *non*allocation of indirect costs to products. Hence, the income statement used internally to evaluate the plant's performance matches directs costs against associated revenues, and then presents indirect costs as separate, lump sum line items. This contribution margin approach focuses management's attention on items it controls while simplifying and refining the reporting process in the plant.

The Controller's objective is to focus the accounting system on planning and control. Managers budget overhead items, and then use direct costs to control operations. The standards used to set flexible budget targets are based on ever-tightening rolling averages of actual costs. Boyer summarizes the management philosophy related to business reports in the following way:

Why poison our outlook with full costs? We focus on controllable factors at the reporting level for managers. Putting overhead in broad buckets facilitates forecasting. Volume-based accounting measures are still used in forecasting and planning... We look for a pure control approach. Namely, for each level of reporting we focus on control and traceability... What we'd like to do is look at the business. We know the variable costs, and know the profit percentages we can make on these items, therefore we know how much we can afford in overhead. Our reporting system focuses on identifying those items we can change. At the top level there's little that can be done to direct costs (although on the plant floor these can be cut), but we do need to keep an eye on overhead items.

Checkbooks and Process Control

The philosophy noted above carries onto the production floor through the use of what management refers to as "checkbooks." These reports are maintained at the lowest level possible within the plant. An example checkbook is shown in Figure 4-3.

The objective behind the development of checkbooks was to communicate to production supervisors their cost constraints. Each report is based on production in a particular department, with finished goods generating revenue-based deposits to the supervisor's "account." These credits are offset by deductions for direct materials, direct labor, set-ups, and other direct costs incurred in producing the products. The supervisor is given great latitude in managing his or her department, subject to the constraint that all scheduled production must be completed on time.

Supervisors are allowed to "save" for future expenses. Additionally, should a department exceed its budget for a certain level of output, the supervisor must immediately request additional funds from the plant manager. This forces a discussion of problems long before traditional cost accounting reports would be available, and enhances the communication process in the plant.

Checkbooks are balanced on a weekly basis, and status reports are generated for each department. This allows the supervisor to verify his or her charges, and to make any changes deemed necessary to current operations to prevent cost overruns. The checkbook approach supports Stanadyne's drive to change its accounting and management philosophy from that of a job shop to a process-oriented JIT facility.

Required:

(1) What are the strengths and weaknesses of the new control reports developed by Stanadyne?

(2) What changes could be made to improve the process control system?

(3) Are these reports compatible with JIT manufacturing? Could they be used in a traditional manufacturing setting?

FIGURE 4-1

Business Report
(000 $)

	Total	Pump	Nozzle	Filter	Other
Net Sales –OEM	2,000	1,000	500	200	300
–SERVICE	2,000	1,500	300	100	100
Total Net Sales	4,000	2,500	800	300	400
Direct Costs					
Material –OEM	800	400	150	100	150
–Service	700	500	100	50	50
–Variance	10	10	(10)	5	5
Total Material	1,510	910	240	155	205
Factory –OEM	725	400	200	75	50
–Service	525	300	100	75	50
–Variance	30	10	10	5	5
Total Factory	1,280	710	310	155	105
Direct Profit	1,210	880	250	(10)	90
Direct Profit %	30.3%	35.2%	31.3%	–3.3%	22.5%
Factory Overhead	300				
Selling & Admin.	100				
Engineering	100				
Tappet	50				
LIFO Setup	10				
Europe P/L	(2)				
Miscellaneous	252				
Income Before Taxes	400				
Return on Sales	10.0%				

FIGURE 4-2

Income Statement

Income Statement by Products	Dollar Amounts in Thousands			
	Total	O.E.	Service	Parts
Sales –Outside	7,500	2,500	2,500	2,500
–Subsidiary	0	0	0	0
–Intra/Inter/Subsidiary	0	0	0	0
–Returns/Allowances/Cash				
Disc.	0	0	0	0
Net Sales	7,500	2,500	2,500	2,500
Standard Cost of Sales				
Material Costs	750	250	250	250
Factory Costs	750	250	250	250
Non-Factory Costs	75	25	25	25
Total STD Variable Costs	1,575	525	525	525
Managed Factory	750	250	250	250
Managed Non-Factory	750	250	250	250
Committed	75	25	25	25
Total STD MGD/COMM	1,575	525	525	525
Income Per Estimate Card	4,350	1,450	1,450	1,450
Variances:				
Difference Replacement &				
Book Depr.	75	25	25	25
Lifo/Inv. Adj. Inflation	(75)	(25)	(25)	(25)
Inv. Discount/Selling				
Adj/Mps/Etc.	(75)	(25)	(25)	(25)
Total	(75)	(25)	(25)	(25)
Volume: Managed –Factory	75	25	25	25
–Non-Factory	(75)	(25)	(25)	(25)
Committed	75	25	25	25
Total Volume Variance	75	25	25	25
Estimate Card Variances	(75)	(25)	(25)	(25)
Spending: Variable –Material	75	25	25	25
–Factory	(75)	(25)	(25)	(25)
–Non-Factory	75	25	25	25
Managed –Factory	(75)	(25)	(25)	(25)
Non-Factory	75	25	25	25
Committed	(75)	(25)	(25)	(25)
Total Spending Variance	0	0	0	0
Operating Income Contribution	4,275	1,425	1,425	1,425
Reserve and Inventory Adjustment				
Royalties Received	0	0	0	0
Capital Employed Income or				
Expense	75	25	25	25
Main Office Exp. ($584,000)				
Operating Income	4,350	1,450	1,450	1,450

FIGURE 4-3
Cell Control Checkbook

Department 350
Prepared by _____

Vendor Name	Req. No.	Date Ordered	Part Number	Furnace Number	Qty. OD	Total Cost
Gas/Salts/Oils	Blank	10/01/86		All	0	18,910.00
Baskets/Liners	Blank	10/01/86		All	0	3,795.50
Advanced ATM	78711	10/13/86	Carbon	Probes	3	2,345.00
Industronics	78714	10/13/86	Alnor	Cards	12	268.00
Kulas	78715	10/13/86	Type K	29″	8	145.50
Kulas	78715	10/13/86	Type K	Wire	1	132.00
Kulas	78715	10/13/86	Type K	18 × 36	4	368.75
Penn/Stokes	78716	10/13/86	V Lube	Vacuums	1	520.50
W.H. Barton	78718	10/13/86	Cooling	Chamber	1	1,680.00
W.W. Graingers	78719	10/13/86	Locks	Crib	6	38.00
Pittsburg	78720	10/13/86	Department	Paint	12	301.00
Sherwin/Will	78721	10/13/86	Department	Paint	4	289.50
Sherwin/Will	78721	10/13/86	Plastic	Buckets	6	102.00
W.W. Graingers	78723	10/24/86	Float	Assembly	2	28.00
					60	(28,923.75)
						30,052.68

Opening Balance

Ending Balance $ 1,128.93

Case 5

Stanadyne Diesel Systems (B)

We've been running off direct costs for several years now. When we were faced with crisis, it was the best way to go. But now, as volumes pick up, I'm concerned about not knowing what it really costs, on a full cost basis, to make our products. How can I make sure we are covering our costs?

Mike Boyer, Controller
Stanadyne Diesel Systems

Background

Standadyne Diesel Systems has undertaken a revolutionary change to its internal reporting system in response to competitive pressures and the demands of supporting a Just-in-Time manufacturing environment. The system, described in case (A), is focused on control. Indirect costs are not allocated to products, but are reported based on lines of responsibility. This informal system has recently been sanctioned by corporate management.

Reminiscent of the direct cost versus full cost controversies of the 1960s, Mike Boyer, Stanadyne's Controller, is wrestling with the tradeoffs made earlier in changing to direct costing. The approach he is taking, rather than moving away from the control-oriented system described earlier, is focused on developing different cost systems for different purposes.

The mentality of the accounting group at Stanadyne is that they provide a service that extends beyond basic report writing, detailed transaction analysis, and issuance of monthly socrecards. An active group, they consider the key questions guiding their efforts to be: Do you know what you are doing? Why? What are you measuring? Developing a good plan and thinking about the information needed both to manage ongoing operations and to support strategic decision-making are key priorities in this group.

The Controller's Problem

Although the Controller's proactive role in the organization is one of the factors contributing to the turnaround at Stanadyne, several issues have recently been raised within the accounting group. The Chief Cost Accountant summarized his view as follows:

> I'm not particularly in favor of decoupling the management accounting system from the financial. I think we would benefit most from an integrated approach, one which factors in both managerial and financial reporting requirements.

One system or two? This is one area of controversy in the firm as the tensions between financial and managerial reporting requirements are brought to the surface.

Stanadyne has been maintaining, separate from the management reporting system, an elaborate system of cost pools to support full cost inventory valuation. In full cost reports, indirect costs — which are not assigned to production in the management reports — are allocated to the various products. Operating decisions are made using direct costs, but Boyer continues to use full costs in answering Marketing's requests for pricing information. Marketing, then, receives both direct cost information in the management reports, and full cost numbers.

The problem facing the Controller arises from this dual system. Overhead tracking, which has been decoupled from the management reporting system, is performed in a corner—the realm of the cost accountant. The control and pricing support functions of overhead reporting are separated under this arrangement. More serious, though, is the increasing tendency by Marketing to use the control reports in making pricing decisions rather than the full cost numbers provided by accounting. Pricing below full cost is thus becoming a routine practice rather than a conscious decision made on the basis of detailed profitability analysis.

Activity Accounting

The full cost versus direct cost argument brings Stanadyne full circle in this controversial area. Many accountants believe that full cost profit margins are the appropriate measure of product line profitability in today's manufacturing environment, due to increasingly large pools of indirect costs. This is essentially the realization being voiced by Boyer. However, he does not consider a return to traditional methods of cost allocation to be a viable option:

> The detail on our fully absorbed cost statements is a problem. I would like to be able to track indirect costs to products, and I want those costs to be accurate. In fact, if we can't make good decisions from the product line statement, then why prepare it? But tracking overhead costs—well, we just don't have a good idea of what causes them.

This is a familiar concern among practicing accountants. The movement to identify and use cost drivers in the tracking and assignment of overhead costs arose partly from the recognition that full costs are more important than ever. Activity accounting has tremendous appeal in this setting—at least at the conceptual level. But how can a company with limited resources find the expertise, time, and money to design and implement such a system? Despite these questions, the Controller has decided to begin a study of activity accounting at Stanadyne.

The basic framework being used in the study is shown in Figure 5-1. Each individual in the overhead group is being asked to list the basic activities that he or she performs, to state what inputs are required and what outputs result from each activity, and finally, to estimate activity time and frequency of occurrence. Combined with payroll data, the beginnings of a database can be constructed, as suggested by Figure 5-2.

The objective is to provide a flexible database of activities that can be accessed on multiple dimensions to support operating decisions, pricing, and ad hoc reporting requirements. The question of what is cost can be approached differently depending on the use to be made of the information. One such use is to identify those activities which add value to the company's products and those which do not.

Potential Problems

The move toward white collar accountability at Stanadyne and other companies underscores the appropriateness of the JIT philosophy—the continuous elimination of waste in the process of value added manufacturing—for factory support activities as well as production activities. However, activity accounting for overhead workers requires some form of time/cost reporting on an ongoing basis. These workers typically have not been held directly accountable for their use of time. Stanadyne personnel are predictably concerned about the outcome of the activity accounting project, as reflected in this comment by Boyer:

> Our people are nervous—and stressed. We're looking to add to this tension, and it may be the straw that breaks the camel's back. They will think it's another way to cut out more people, and they won't want to cooperate. Sure we need the information, but I just don't know if we can get it without damaging the fragile relationships we have with our people.

This is an interesting challenge. Several forms of dysfunctional behavior have been detected in public accounting, where time-based reporting has been used for years. These include overstating the time spent on tasks, shifting time from one task to another, and reporting as completed tasks that were never undertaken.

The critical issue may be how the information is used. If its use is restricted to product cost measurement and inventory valuation, people will have little incentive to misreport. But if the data are used for control and performance evaluation purposes, some falsification of reports may be expected. Finally, if the data are used to "weed out" individuals doing non-value added work, the accountant may be considered by some employees to be acting as their judge and potential executioner.

The concept of activity accounting is intuitively appealing, suggesting overhead costs can be analyzed and traced based on the activities that cause them. Implementing the concept, however, is far from simple. It requires a change in mindset among indirect labor groups, and a defined level of accountability not found in many existing systems. If used improperly, it could serve to divide, rather than to support and integrate, the people in an organization. As a new approach to cost analysis, activity accounting needs to be closely examined for both its benefits and its potential dangers.

Required:

(1) Is direct costing information appropriate for operating decisions? For pricing decisions?

(2) What problems are firms likely to encounter as they attempt to structure and implement activity accounting systems? What is your opinion of the approach being used by Stanadyne?

(3) Should the management accounting system consist of one integrated database, or should separate cost systems be developed for different purposes?

(4) Should accountants assume the role of reporting value added and non-value added activities? Why or why not?

FIGURE 5-1

Framework for Activity Accounting Study

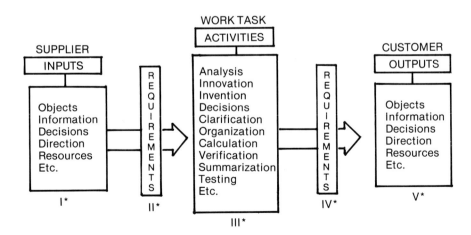

*Summary of the Model: All work may be thought of as occurring within a system. The System involves the "Supplier" providing inputs (I) based upon sets of requirements (II) to the "Work Task" (III) and its activities. The activities of the work task add value to the work and make it conform to other requirements (IV) before providing it as an output (V) to the "Customer."

FIGURE 5-2

Chargeback System

A chargeback system is both an accounting process to monitor resource usage and a mechanism for attaching the costs of these resources to the activities and/or products they support. McKinnon and Kallman (1987) suggest that a complete chargeback system should:

1. Record usage at a level that identifies all resources consumed.

2. Identify the individual performing the work as well as the process, product, or department receiving benefit.

3. Summarize usage based on classifications that impart the greatest amount of information (i.e., match the information use). The focus is on not only dollars expended but also the type of resource consumed and the level of service provided.

4. Report the summarized usage at regular intervals to identify significant trends and characteristics.

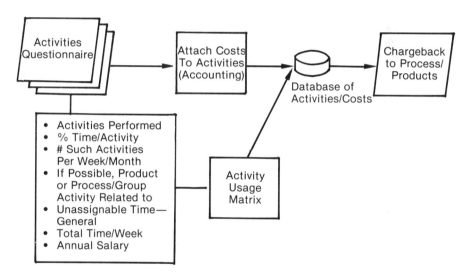

National Association of Accountants
Committee on Academic Relations
1988-89

Chairman
Murlin C. Barker, CPA
President
Green Tree Business Consultants
San Marino, CA

Mr. John G. Baab, CPA
Partner
Ernst & Whinney
Grand Rapids, MI

Mr. Robert L. Barber, CMA
Director of Financial Services
Moses H. Cone Memorial Hospital
Greensboro, NC

Dr. James W. Brackner, CPA
Associate Professor
School of Accountancy
Utah State University
Logan, UT

Ms. Margaret D. Butler, CPA
Assistant Controller
Super Valu Stores, Inc.
Atlanta, GA

Dr. Edwin H. Caplan, CPA
Dean
The Robert O. Anderson
   Schools of Management
University of New Mexico
Albuquerque, NM

Mr. Robert A. Czekanski, CMA
Division Controller
Squibb Company
New Brunswick, NJ

Dr. Dale L. Flesher, CMA, CPA
Professor of Accounting
School of Accountancy
University of Mississippi
University, MS

Mr. Robert W. Green, CMA
Assistant Treasurer
Ebasco Services Incorporated
New York, NY

Mr. David F. McCormick, CPA
Defense Contract Audit Agency
Southwestern Region
Los Angeles, CA

Dr. Charles D. Mecimore, CMA, CPA
Professor of Accounting
Head, Department of Accounting
University of North Carolina – Greensboro
Greensboro, NC

Mr. Gail L. Nash
Comptroller
Arizona Department of Transportation
Phoenix, AZ

Dr. Michael A. Robinson
Associate Professor of Accounting
Department of Accounting
Abilene Christian University
Abilene, TX

Dr. Harold P. Roth, CMA, CPA
Associate Professor of Accounting
Department of Accounting and
    Business Law
University of Tennessee
Knoxville, TN

Dr. Carl Smith, CMA, CPA
Assistant Professor of Accounting
Department of Accounting
University of Hartford
West Hartford, CT

Ms. Claudia P. Spencer, CPA
Senior Manager
BDO Seidman
Beverly Hills, CA

Dr. Manuel A. Tipgos, CPA
Professor of Accounting
School of Accountancy
University of Kentucky
Lexington, KY

Dr. Curtis C. Verschoor, CMA, CIA,
    CPA
Professor of Accounting
School of Accountancy
DePaul University
Chicago, IL

Ms. Kim R. Wallin, CPA
Partner
DK Wallin, Ltd.
Las Vegas, NV

Mr. James D. Wilson
Corporate Controller
Martin Industries, Inc.
Florence, AL

Dr. Robert B. Sweeney
MSU Chair of Accountancy
Fogelman College of Business
    & Economics
Memphis State University
Memphis, TN

Committee Staff

Ms. Hadassah Slominsky, CMA, CPA
Manager – Academic Relations
National Association of Accountants
10 Paragon Drive
Montvale, NJ 07645-1760
Office Phone: (201) 573-6306
Staff Secretary

Dr. James Bulloch, CMA, CPA
Managing Director
Institute of Certified Management
    Accountants and Professional
        Relations
10 Paragon Drive
Montvale, NJ 07645-1759
Office Phone: (201) 573-6192